Theory Time!

Step by Step Instructions for ABRSM and Other Exams

Grade 1

by

DAVID TURNBULL

CONTENTS

Bosworth

THEORY TIME!

Grade 1

The purpose of these books is to teach the principles of music theory. They are intended not only for pupils who want to pass theory examinations, but also for all those who would like to learn something about the theory of music as part of their general education. This book covers the syllabus of Grade 1 of the Associated Board.

The sections of the book explain the ideas you need to know, and test your understanding with frequent questions. Write down your answers to these questions in the spaces provided, and then look up the printed answers.

You will notice that answers to questions are always printed on different pages from the questions themselves. The answers to Page 1 questions are in the margin of Page 2, for example, and the answers to Page 2 questions are in the margin of Page 1. Make sure that you look up the printed answers *only* after you have written down your own if you want to make good progress.

You can use this book with your teacher, who can set you pages to work through and then explain any difficulties you may have. Or you can use it to teach yourself. You can also use it for revision.

The sections of the book deal with different aspects of theory, but you need not work through to the end of each section before going on to the next. Your teacher may wish to recommend a different order of working – for example, part of Section 1, then part of Section 2 before returning to complete Section 1. However, it is recommended that you should finish this book before you go on to Grade 2.

Past examination papers are published by the Associated Board of the Royal Schools of Music and can be used for further practice, as can the series of books *Music Theory in Practice*, by Eric Taylor, also published by the Associated Board.

David Turnbull
Solihull, England, 1994

For Further Reference and Practice:

Reference
> **The AB Guide to Music Theory, Part 1.** Eric Taylor. Published by the Associated Board of the Royal Schools of Music. London 1989. An extremely comprehensive and reliable reference book.

THEORY TIME! GRADE 1

Section 1 –Time

Answers to questions on this page are in the margin of Page 2

Answers to Page 2 questions

notes

1 Look at these notes:

	stem		stem		
♩	head	♩	head	o	head

They have oval **heads**. The first has a 'black' head — an oval outline filled in. The second and third have 'white' heads — the oval outline is black but the inside of the oval is white. The first and second notes have **stems** as well as heads.

5(a) too big; (b) too small; (c) head spreads outside space; (d) line must go through middle of note; (e) correct

crotchet

♩

2 The first note is called a **crotchet**, and it is the note we meet most often at first. Americans call a crotchet a *quarter-note.* In Grade 1 work, we use the crotchet to measure the length of all our notes and rests. In this grade, **one crotchet is worth one beat.**

minim

♩

3 The second note is called a **minim** *(American — half-note)*. It has a white head, a stem, and no tail. It lasts twice as long as a crotchet. How many crotchet beats is it worth? _____

6(a)   (b)   (c)

semibreve

o

4 The third note is called a **semibreve** *(American — whole note)*. It has a white head, and no stem. It lasts twice as long as a minim. How many crotchet beats is it worth? _____

TEST 1

(a) Draw a note worth 1 beat here:_____(b) Draw a note worth 4 beats here:_____

(c) What is the length of this note? **o** _____

(d) What is the length of this note? ♩ _____

(e) How many crotchets last as long as one minim? _____

(f) A semibreve lasts as long as how many minims?_____

(g) A minim is how many times as long as a crotchet? _____

(h) A semibreve is how many times as long as a crotchet?_____

How many of your answers were correct? _____ If you got less than 8 right, revise paragraphs 1-4 and do the test a second time.

**notes heads
on a stave**

5 So far we have written notes on unlined paper, but music is usually written on a five-line stave. We have to write the note heads on a stave very carefully.

Either the note head must be written on a line, with the line going *exactly* through the middle of the note head,

or the note head must be written in the space between two lines, and must not go outside this space.

Tick those of the following which are correct. Rewrite those that are wrong.

stems

6 Notice the direction of stems on the stave.

- notes **below** the middle line have stems going **up** from the **right** of the note;

- notes **above** the middle line have stems going **down** from the **left** of the note;

- notes **on** the middle line may have their stems going **up or down.**

Correct any wrongly drawn notes. Tick those which are correct.

Other points to note about stems:

- Make sure that your stems touch the heads.

- Draw the stems at right angles to the staff

- Length of stems should be about three spaces.

3 2 beats

4 4 beats

TEST 1 (a) ♩ (b) 𝅝

(c) 4 beats; (d) 2 beats;
(e) 2; (f) 2
(g) twice;
(h) four times

Answers to Page 4 Questions
11a

b

Mark with a tick correctly drawn notes below. Write the correct version to the right of any you think are wrong.

(g)　　　(h)　　　(i)　　　(j)　　　(k)

In 2-4 we learned about 1-beat notes (crotchets,) 2-beat notes (minims) and 4-beat notes (semibreves). Now we must learn about notes worth less than a crotchet.

quaver

7 The **quaver** has a filled-in head, a stem, and also a **tail**.

The quaver is half as long as a crotchet. The American name for a quaver is an *eighth note*. How many quavers equal the length of

(a) a crotchet? _____ (b) a minim? _____ (c) a semibreve? _____

beaming of quavers

8 Quavers may be joined together into groups by their tails, which become a thick line called a **beam**. Notes joined together like this are said to be **beamed**.

13 3

Don't beam more than two quavers together for now – in other words, the total length of the beamed group should not be more than one beat.

Rewrite correctly beamed: (a) _____

14 2

(b) _____

semiquaver

9 The semiquaver has a filled-in head, a stem, and a **double** tail. It is half as long as a quaver, so it is worth a quarter of a beat - four semi-quavers last as long as one crotchet. Americans call a semiquaver a *sixteenth note*. How many semiquavers equal the length of (a) a minim? _____ (b) a semibreve? _____

beaming of semi-quavers

10 Like quavers, semiquavers may be beamed. As there are two tails to be joined together, there are two beams.

15(a) 2; (b) 1; (c) 4; (d) 2 (e) 4

Don't beam more than four semiquavers together for now.

Rewrite correctly beamed: (a) _____

(b) _____

**Answers to
Page 3
Questions**

6(g) too short; (h) not at
right angle; (i) not
touching head; (j) too
long; (k) correct.

7(a) 2; (b) 4; (c) 8

8(a)

(b)

9(a) 8; (b) 16

10(a)

(b)

**beaming
mixed
groups of
quavers
and semi-
quavers**

11 You may beam groups containing both quavers and semiquavers up to the value of one beat.

Write these notes out again with correct beaming
(a)   (b)

rests

12 As well as being able to show the number of beats for which notes sound, we must also be able to measure the length of silences, known as **rests**. Each note has a rest of the same value.

**crotchet
rest**

13 The crotchet rest can be drawn by writing a z on its side, and under it a c. Practise drawing a row.

How many beats are these rests worth in total?   _____

minim rest

14 The minim rest is written as an oblong block which stands on the middle line of the staff - the third line from the top.

To how many crotchet rests is it equal? _____

**semibreve
rest**

15 The semibreve rest is written as an oblong block that hangs from the second line down of the staff.

As its shape is the same as a minim rest, and the only difference is where it is placed, it is easy to confuse minim and semibreve rests. You may find it helpful to remember that

- the **m**inim rest stands on the **m**iddle line
- the **se**mibreve rest hangs from the **se**cond line

How many beats are these worth?

(a)_____ (b)_____ (c)_____ (d)_____ (e)_____

Answers to
Page 6
questions

quaver rest

16 The quaver rest is written on the stave like this – practise writing three more.

It is worth half a crotchet beat. so to how many beats (and parts of a beat) are these rests worth? ╕ ╕ ╕ _____

TEST 3.
(j) (k) (l) (m) (n)

(o) (p) (q) (r) (s)

semiquaver rest

17 The semiquaver rest is written like this, with two tails. It is worth a quarter of a beat.

To how many beats (and parts of a beat) are these rests equal? ⅔ ╕ ⅔
_____

TEST 2 Write single rests worth
(a) ½ beat;   (b) 4 beats;   (c) ¼ beat;   (d) 2 beats;   (e) 1 beat

If you made any mistakes, read over 12 - 17 again.

---

dotted notes and rests

18 A note or a rest is made longer by putting a dot after it. The dot **adds half the length of the original note or rest.**

This is a minim followed by a dot. A minim is worth 2 beats. The dot will add half the original length. Half of 2 beats is 1 beat so the length of a dotted minim will be 2 beats + 1 beat = 3 beats.

This is a dotted crotchet rest. A crotchet rest is worth 1 beat. The dot adds half of one beat, which is a half. The total length of the dotted crotchet rest will be 1 beat + ½ beat = 1½ beats.

BEWARE! Beginners often think wrongly that a dot adds **half a beat** to a dotted note. This is *only* the case if the note is a one-beat note - **the dot adds one half the original value, whatever it may be .**

What is the value of this note?   o.   _____

19(a) 5 beats (four for the semibreve and 1 for the crotchet).
(b) 1½ beats (1 for the crotchet and ½ for the quaver).
(c) 4 beats (2 for each minim).

(d)   (e)   (f)

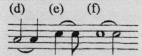

TEST 3 Write down the number of crotchet beats (or parts of a beat) the following are worth:

(a)____(b)____(c)____(d)____(e)____(f)____(g)____(h)____(i)____

Test 3 continued on Page 6

Answers to questions on this page are in the margin of Page 5

TEST 3
(continued)

Write on the stave single notes worth the following:
(j) 6 beats; (k) ¾ beat; (l) 3 beats; (m) 1½ beats (n) 3/8 of a beat

Write single rests on the stave worth the following:
(o) 3 beats; p) 1½ beats q) 3/8 beat (r) 6 beats (s) ¾ beat

Write here the number of your correct answers. _____ If you made more than two mistakes, read 18 again and do the test once more.

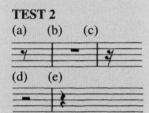
tied notes

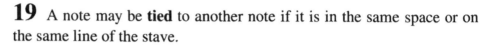

19 A note may be **tied** to another note if it is in the same space or on the same line of the stave.

The second note isn't sounded separately. Instead, its value is added on to the first note.

In the example, a minim is tied to a crotchet. The value of the crotchet is added to the minim, so the total length of sound will be three beats – two for the minim and one for the tied crotchet.

The tie is written as a curved line between the two note heads. The tie sign goes **above** the note heads if the stems go down, but **below** the note heads which have stems which go up.

Write down the number of beats the sound will last of

(a)_____ (b)_____ (c)_____

Rewrite using ties instead of dots to give the same rhythm:
(d) (e) (f)

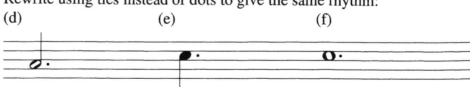

Notice that rests are never tied

bars

20 Music is usually written in **bars** *(American - measures)*. A bar is the space between one **barline** and the next.

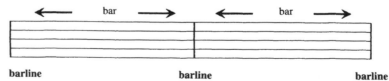

barline   barline   barline

Answers to Page 8 questions

The last barline of a piece is written as a *double* barline, to show that the end has been reached.

The notes of each bar add up to a certain number of crotchet beats.

How many crotchet beats are there in each of the following bars?

(a) _____beats   (b) _____beats   (c)_____beats

Usually, each bar in a piece, or section of a piece, will contain the same number of beats.

23 simple quadruple

time signatures

21 The number of beats in each bar of the piece is shown at the beginning by the **time signature.** A time signature has two numbers, one above the other, like these: **¾ 4/4**

24(a) 3
(b) Yes
(c) No – put one in
(d) No. Bars 3 and 4 are complete.

The **top** number of the time signature tells you the number of beats there are in each bar.

How many beats are there in the bar if the time signature is

(a) **4/4** _____ (b) **2/4** ?_____ (c) **3/4** ?_____

The **bottom** number is a code which tells you what sort of note is used as the beat. The code number for **crotchet** beats is 4. This is because four crotchet beats are equal in length to a semibreve.

4/4 tells you that there are 4 crotchet beats in each bar.

2/4 tells you that there are two crotchet beats in each bar.

All the time signatures you will meet in Grade 1 will have 4 as the bottom figure, as the crotchet is always used as the beat in this grade.

What time signature will tell you that there are

(d) three crotchet beats to the bar? _____

(e) 5 crotchet beats to the bar? _____

TEST 4
1(a) **4/4** or **C**; (b) **¾** ;
(c) **2/4** ; (d) **4/4** or **C**
(e) **¾** (f) **¾** (g) **2/4**
2(a)
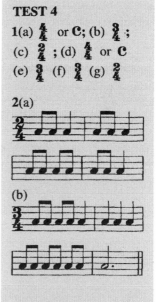
3(a) simple duple
(b) simple triple

common time

C

22 The time signature you will meet most often is **4/4** - four crotchet beats to the bar.

4/4 time is called **common time**, and the time signature for it can be written as **C** instead of **4/4** .

7

time names **23** If there are **four** beats in the bar, the time is called **simple quad-ruple** time.
If there are **three** beats in the bar, the time is called **simple triple** time.
If there are **two** beats in the bar, the time is called **simple duple** time.

What sort of time is **C** ?_____

insertion of barlines **24** You may have to put missing barlines into melodies.
Look at this example, and work through the stages below:

(a) How many beats should there be in each bar?_____

(b) Start at the beginning, and count the beats until you get to where the first bar should end. Is there a bar line in place? _____

(c) Count until you get to where the second bar should end. Is there a bar line present? _____ If not, write one in.

(d) Continue in this way through each bar until you reach the end of the melody. Are any other bar lines missing? _____

TEST 4 Write at the beginning of these bars their time signatures:
1(a)   (b)   (c)   (d)

(e)   (f)   (g)

2 Put in any missing barlines in these melodies;
(a)

(b)

3 Name the time (simple duple, etc.) of 2(a) _____

2(b)_____

Write down the number of correct answers _____ If it was less than 9, read 21-24 again, and do the test once more

8

Answers to Page 10 Questions

completion of bars

25 You will often have to complete bars which do not have their full number of beats. Whenever doing work of this sort, **pencil in the main beats over the top of the bar.**

i. by adding a beat

For example, you may be asked to complete the following bar by adding a note at *

(a) Look at the time signature. How many complete beats should there be in each bar? **Pencil them in over the top of the bar.**

(b) How many beats are already present in the bar? _____

(c) How many beats will have to be put in at * to make up the number needed by the time signature? _____

(d) What is the missing note? _____ Write it in.

ii. by adding part of a beat

26 You may need to complete a bar by putting in parts of a beat, either with notes or a rest. Look at the bar below.

(a) How many complete beats should there be in  this bar? _____

(b) **Pencil over the top of the bar the main beats.**

(c) Using these pencilled main beats to help you, decide which beat is incomplete. Which beat in this bar needs to be completed? _____

(d) How much of the beat is missing? _____

(e) Put in the note which will complete it.

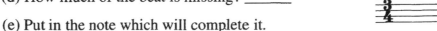

iii. by adding a rest

27 Rests can be used to complete bars.

(a) how many beats should there be? _____

Pencil in these beats over the top of the bar.

(b) how many beats are present already? _____

(c) how many beats rest must be put in? _____

(d) write in the missing rest at *

whole bar rest

28 If there are no notes at all in a bar, a semibreve rest must be written. Notice that a semibreve rest is *always* used, whether the bar is four beats long, three beats long or two beats long.

Write in a rest to complete the bar at *

Answers to Page 10 Questions

TEST 5

29 c is wrong. The quavers of beat 2 are joined to beat 3.

9

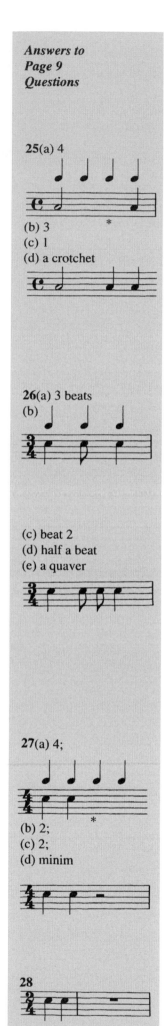

25(a) 4

(b) 3
(c) 1
(d) a crotchet

26(a) 3 beats
(b)

(c) beat 2
(d) half a beat
(e) a quaver

27(a) 4;

(b) 2;
(c) 2;
(d) minim

28

Answers to questions on this page are in the margin of Page 9

TEST 5 1. Complete each of the following bars with a single note:

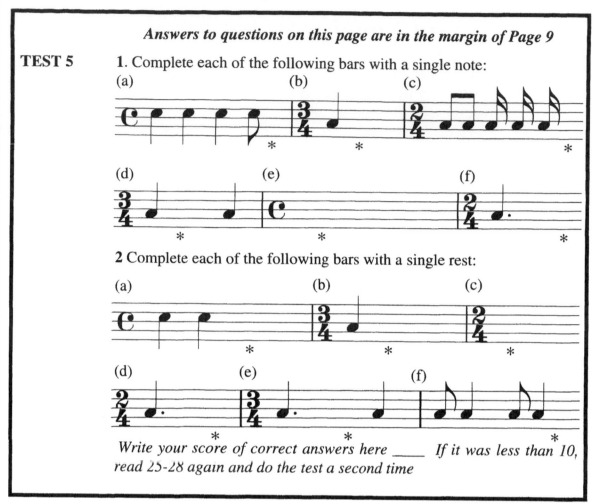

2 Complete each of the following bars with a single rest:

Write your score of correct answers here ____ If it was less than 10, read 25-28 again and do the test a second time

More about beaming quavers

29 In Sections 8 and 10 you learned how to beam together quavers. So far, you have beamed these notes together in pairs. But you may sometimes also beam quavers together in longer groups.

i. In **common time** quavers and may be joined together if they make up the **first two beats** or the **last two beats** of the bar.

Which of the following is wrong? _____
(a)   (b)   (c)

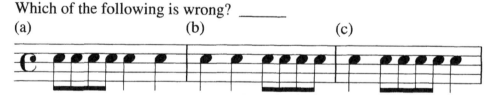

ii. If quavers make up a complete bar of either ²/₄ time or ³/₄ time, they may be joined together.

Rewrite, beaming quavers correctly:

(d)

10

writing your own rhythms

30 In Grade 1, you will be given the rhythm of the first two bars of a four-bar phrase, and then asked to complete the rhythm of the phrase.

The phrase, once completed, must sound musical to listeners, and above all to you, the composer. There are many ways of completing a phrase musically, but here are some suggestions which will work well.

Here is a two-bar rhythm - tap it over.

To complete it in the simplest possible way, first compose a rhythm for bar 3. It is a good idea to use the same rhythm as bar 1, or one very like it. So now the first three bars of the phrase could be

1(1) Lower

Now add a fourth bar. It can be different from bar 2 above. Finish with a note not less than one beat in length. Clap what you have written.

(2) 3

(3) 2

Here are more two-bar phrases for you to complete:

(a)

(b)

(c)

2 8

(d)

Section 2 - Pitch

Answers to questions on this page are in the margin of Page 11

the keyboard

1 Look at this diagram of part of a keyboard.

There are white notes and black notes on the keyboard. We will learn about the white notes first.

Notes rise in **pitch** (get higher in sound) from left to right of the keyboard.

1(1) Is note 1 higher or lower in pitch than note 2? _____

white notes and black notes

Look at the notes in the diagram. Start from the left. Group 1 has four white notes.
1(2) How many black notes are there between them? _____

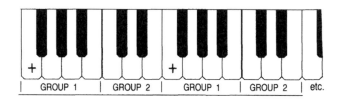

Then there is a Group 2 of three white notes.
1(3) How many black notes are there between the white notes? _____

Groups 1 and 2 are repeated.

the octave

2 The lowest note of the first Group 1 and the lowest note of the second Group 1 are marked with crosses, + +

Including the crossed notes in your counting, how many white notes are there between the crosses? _____

We call a distance of eight notes an **octave**. Notes an octave apart sound so much like each other that they have the same name.

names of white notes

3 White notes are named after the first seven letters of the alphabet - A, B, C, D, E. F, and G. We use capital letters. The two notes with crosses above are both called F.

12

Answers to questions on this page are in the margin of Page 14

To find A on the keyboard, look at Group 1. Find the third white note of the group. This is A. There are two As in the next diagram, an octave apart.

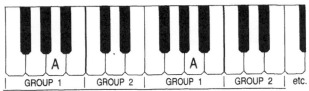

What is the name of the white note to the right of A? ___

white notes on the keyboard

4 Once we know the name of one note, we can work out the names of all the other white notes on the diagram. Remember that the white notes are A, B, C, D, E, F and G. Then we have the next A.
Which note names are missing from the diagram? _____ Write them in.

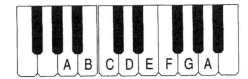

Now we must find out how these notes are written on music paper.

the stave

5 Music is written on a five-line **stave**. Notes are written on lines or in spaces.

Look at the note which is written on the second line up.

The note **above** it in pitch is written in the space between the second line and the middle line. The note **below** it in pitch is in the space between the bottom two lines.

clefs

6 Each stave starts with a sign called a **clef.** Using a clef, we can work out the names of the notes on the stave. For Grade 1 we have to know two clefs, the **treble clef** and the **bass** clef.

treble clef

7 The treble clef is often called the 'G' clef. It starts with part of a circle round the second line up of the stave. Any note written on this line is the note G.

Practise writing treble clefs.

Answers to questions on Page 14

7 G   A   F

8 (1)   (2)   (3)

(4)   (5)

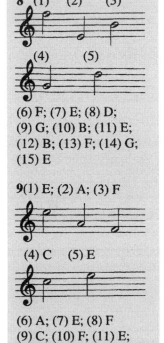

(6) F; (7) E; (8) D;
(9) G; (10) B; (11) E;
(12) B; (13) F; (14) G;
(15) E

9 (1) E; (2) A; (3) F

(4) C   (5) E

(6) A; (7) E; (8) F
(9) C; (10) F; (11) E;
(12) C; (13) E; (14) F;
(15) C

13

The first note in this bar is G.
What are the letter names of the others? _____

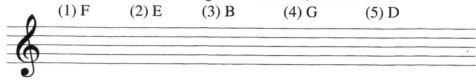

notes on lines

E G B D F

8 Learn the names of notes on lines first. They are E, G, B, D and F. Some people use sentences to help them to remember, like 'Every Good Boy Deserves Food.' Use it, or make one up for yourself.

Write on the stave the following notes on lines, as minims:

(1) F   (2) E   (3) B   (4) G   (5) D

Write below these notes their letter names

(6)___(7)___(8) ___(9) _(10) _(11)__(12)__(13)__(14) _(15)__

9 Now learn the notes in spaces. They spell the word FACE.

Write the following notes, as minims, in spaces on the stave:

(1) E   (2) A   (3) F   (4) C   (5) E

F A C E

notes in spaces

Write below these notes their letter names:

(6)___(7)___(8) ___(9) _(10) _(11)__(12)__(13)__(14) _(15) __

ledger line for middle C

E D C

10 The bottom line of the treble clef stave is used for the note E. The note below E, which is D, is written below the bottom line.

If we want to write the note below D, which is C, we must draw an extra line to put it on. This extra line is called a **ledger line**. *It is short – just long enough to carry the note.*

The C shown is the note in the middle of a piano keyboard, and is called 'middle C'.

Answers to questions on this page are in the margin of Page 16

Write the following notes as crotchets on the stave:
(1) middle C; (2) G on a line; (3) C in a space; (4) G above the stave;
(5) D on a line; (6) D below the stave; (7) B on a line; (8) E in a space;
(9) E on a line; (10) F on a line.

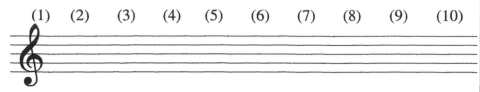

What are the letter names of these notes?

(11)__(12)__(13)__(14)__(15)__(16)__(17)__(18)__(19)__(20)__

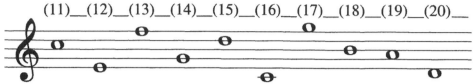

Write your score here ____ If you scored less than 19, read over paragraphs 8-10 again, and do the test once more.

---

bass clef

11 This is often called the 'F' clef. Notice the two dots written above and below the second line from the top. All notes on this line are Fs.

notes on lines

G B D F A

12 The notes on the lines are G, B, D, F and A. Some people remember them by the sentence '**G**reat **B**ig **D**ogs **F**rom **A**frica'. When you know them well, answer the questions below:

Write as crotchets on lines: (1) A; (2) G; (3) D; (4) B; (5) F

Name the following notes:

(6)__ (7)__(8)__(9)__(10)__(11)__(12)__(13)__(14)__(15)__

notes in spaces

13 Learn the notes in the spaces on the left. Some people use the sentence '**A**ll **C**ows **E**at **G**rass' to help them.

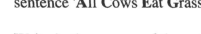

A C E G

Write in the names of the notes below:

(1)__ (2)__ (3)__ (4)__ (5)__(6)__ (7)__ (8)__(9)__ (10)__

15

A   B   Middle C

14 The top line of the bass clef is A. B can be written above it, but if you want to write C you must draw a ledger line. This C is middle C.

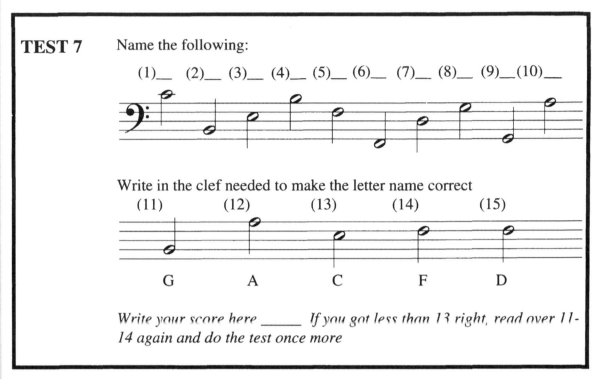

TEST 7   Name the following:

(1)__ (2)__ (3)__ (4)__ (5)__ (6)__ (7)__ (8)__ (9)__(10)__

Write in the clef needed to make the letter name correct

(11)   (12)   (13)   (14)   (15)

G   A   C   F   D

Write your score here _____ If you got less than 13 right, read over 11-14 again and do the test once more

black notes   **15** So far, we have learned about white notes only. Now we must learn the names of the black notes. Look at the diagram of the keyboard:

*

F G A B C D

Look at the white notes F, G, A, C and D. There is a black note to the right of each of these white notes.

sharps   **16** The black note to the right of a white note is called a **sharp.** The black note to the right of F is called F sharp. The black note to the right of G is called G sharp, and so on.

Look at the keyboard in 15.

(1) What is the name of the black note to the right of C? _____

(2) What is the name of the black note to the right of D? _____

The sign for sharp is ♯ .

Answers to Page 18 questions

flats

17 Look at the starred note in the diagram in **15**. It is the black note to the *right* of A. But it is also the black note to the *left* of B

A black note to the left of a white note is called a **flat**. So the note marked * in **15** can be called either A sharp or B flat. The sign for a flat is ♭

Each black note therefore has two names. It can be called the sharp of the white note immediately to its left, or the flat of the white note immediately to its right.

Look at this diagram and complete the following sentences:

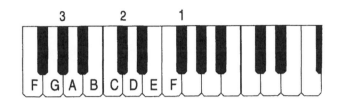

(1) Note 1 is called _____ sharp or _____ flat
(2) Note 2 is called _____ sharp or _____ flat
(3) Note 3 is called _____ sharp or _____ flat

20(1) B flat; (2) A; (3) B flat; (4) B; (5) C

not

Though we write 'F sharp' or 'G flat' in words, when we are writing sharps and flats on the stave we always put the sharp sign or flat sign **in front** of the note.

not

What is the name (4) of the third note in bar 1 and (5) of the third note in bar 2?

(4) _____ (5) _____

21(1) a semitone; (2) raises

(3) flat; (4) flattens

(5) natural

ii. naturals

18 A sharp or a flat sign can be cancelled by using a **natural** sign written like this: ♮ *(Americans sometimes use the term 'cancel sign' for a natural.)* The first note below is A sharp. The second is A natural. Name the others in the line.

(1) A♯ (2) A♮ (3) ____ (4) ____ (5) ____ (6) ____ (7) ____

17

accidentals

19 Sharps, flats and natural signs are called **accidentals.** Notice that they are very carefully written, so that they are *exactly* on the lines or in the spaces of their notes.

20 Once an accidental has been written in front of a note, it continues to sharpen or flatten the note until the end of the bar in which it appears. The example below should make this clear.

In Bar 1, Note 1 is F.

Note 2 is F sharp, because of the accidental in front of it.

Note 3 is *also* F sharp. It doesn't need its own sharp because of the sharp in front of note 2, which lasts throughout the bar.

In Bar 2 Note 4 is F and *not* F sharp, because the sharp sign in front of Note 2 lasts only until the end of bar 1.

Name the notes in the bars below:

(1)_____ (2)_____ (3)_____ (4)_____ (5)_____

17(1) F sharp/G flat
(2) C sharp/D flat
(3) G sharp/A flat

semitones

21 The distance between a note and the next note to it is a **semitone**. It doesn't matter if the note is white or black. Look at this diagram:

The next note to the right of F is F sharp (or G flat) Therefore, the distance from F to F sharp is a semitone.

The next note to the left of F is E. Therefore the distance from F to E is a semitone.

Complete the following:

(1) What is the distance between B and C? _____

(2) The sharp sign in front of a note _____ the note by a semitone.

(3) The _____ sign in front of a note lowers the note by a semitone.

(4) The natural sign in front of a sharpened note _____ the note by a semitone.

(e.) The _____ sign in front of a flattened note raises the note by a semitone.

(4) F sharp
(5) B flat

18(3) B flat;
(4) B natural;
(5) C sharp;
(6) G flat
(7) F

Answers to Page 20 questions

TEST 8
accidentals

1 Write underneath these notes their names. You may use the ♯ and ♭ signs for sharps and flats where necessary.

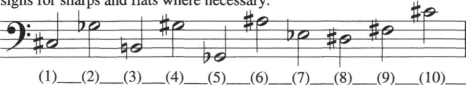

(1)___(2)___(3)___(4)___(5)___(6)___(7)___(8)___(9)___(10)___

2 Using accidentals if necessary, make the second note of each pair a semitone lower than the first note:

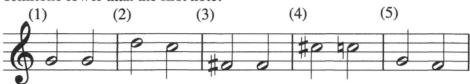

3 Name the numbered notes in this phrase:

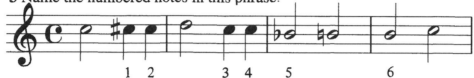

Write your score here_____ If more than two of your answers are wrong read over 16-21 again, and do the test once more.

tones

22 We have seen in 21 that the distance between two notes next to each other is a semitone. Two semitones make **one tone.** Look at the keyboard diagram below:

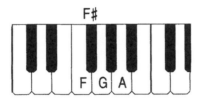

(1) What is the distance between F sharp and G? _____
(2) What is the distance between G and A?_____
The distance between G and A is a tone because there are two semitones between the notes. The first semitone is between G and G sharp, and the second is between G sharp and A. Two semitones make one tone.

intervals

23 The distance between one note and another is called the **interval** between them. We will learn more about intervals later. So far, the intervals we have studied have been the octave, the semitone and the tone.

Section 3
3(a) A;
(b) B;

4(a) a tone;
(b) a semitone
(c) a tone
(d) a tone
(e) a semitone

Section 3 - Scales, Keys, Intervals & Tonic Triads

Answers to questions on this page are in the margin of Page 19

scales

1 A **scale** is a series of notes, arranged in steps in ascending or descending order.

There are several different types of scale in use: **major**, **minor** and **chromatic** scales are the most common. In Grade 1, you need to know about the major scales of G, D and F.

C major

2 Here is the scale of C major. It is made up of the white notes from C to the C an octave above. Play it on a keyboard, and look at the music and the diagram.

Notice that the C at the top of the scale is marked C' so that it isn't confused with the lower C.

degrees of the scale

3 The notes of the scale are called the **degrees** of the scale. Number them from 1 to 7.

keynote

In C major, the first degree - Note 1 - is C. Note 1 of a scale is also called its **keynote**.

The second degree (Note 2) is D; the third degree is E; the fourth degree is F; the fifth degree is G.

(a) What note is Note 6, the sixth degree? ____
(b) What note is Note 7, the seventh degree? _____

tones and semitones in C major

4 Look at the first group of four notes in the scale of C major.

The interval between the first degree of the scale, C (Note 1) and the second degree, D (Note 2) is a tone.

(a) What is the interval between D (Note 2) and E (Note 3)? _____

(b) What is the interval between E (3) and F (4)? _____

Look at the second group of four notes, made up of G, A, B and top C

(c) What is the interval between G (5) and A(6)? _____

(d) What is the interval between A (6) and B (7)? _____

(e) What is the interval between B (7) and C (1')? _____

Answers to Page 22 Questions

5 The scale of C major is made up of two groups of four notes.
In each group the intervals between the notes are Tone-Tone-Semitone.

The groups are linked together by the interval between F (4) and G (5).

Is this linking interval a tone or a semitone? Write the correct answer in the plan below at ↓

First Group.....   ...Link   Second Group

Tone-Tone-Semitone ↓_____ Tone-Tone-Semitone

8(a) a tone
(b) a semitone

major scale intervals

6 In C major, **and in all major scales,**

- there is a **tone** between Notes 1 and 2;
- there is a **tone** between Notes 2 and 3;
- there is a **semitone** between Notes 3 and 4;
- there is a **tone** between Notes 4 and 5;
- there is a **tone** between Notes 5 and 6;
- there is a **tone** between Notes 6 and 7;
- there is a **semitone** between Notes 7 and the top note

Between which notes of a major scale are there semitones? _____

TTS T TTS Learn by heart the intervals between the degrees in major scales: **T**one-**T**one-**S**emitone-**T**one-**T**one-**T**one-**S**emitone. For short, **TTSTTTS**.

7 Look at the white notes from G to the G an octave above.

- Between G (Note 1) and A (Note 2) there is a tone;
- Between A (Note 2) and B (Note 3) there is a tone;
- Between B (Note 3) and C (Note 4) there is a semitone;
- Between C (Note 4) and D (Note 5) there is a tone;
- Between D (Note 5) and E (Note 6) there is a tone;

What is the interval between (a) E (Note 6) and F? _____
(b) F and G'? _____

10(a) C major
(b) G major;
(c) C major

(d)

8 The interval between E (6) and F is a *semitone*. But in major scales the interval between Notes 6 and 7 should be a *tone*.

The interval between F and top G' is a tone. But in major scales the interval between Note 7 and the top note should be a *semitone*.

As we cannot get our correct order by using white notes only, we will have to use a black note.

If we use F *sharp* instead of F as 7

(a) what is the interval between E (6) and F sharp (7)? _____

(b) what is the interval between F sharp and the top note, G'? _____

By choosing F sharp instead of F, we have kept to our TTSTTTS order for a major scale. Here is G major scale, with brackets over the semitones:

9 We learned in Section **2.17** that a black note has two names: it is the sharp of the white note to its left, and the flat of the white note to its right.

We have to decide why Note 7 in G major is called F sharp and not G flat.

The reason is that in a scale all the letters of the alphabet from A to G must appear once, as a natural or a sharp or a flat note.

If we had called 7 G flat instead of F sharp, there would be no F in our scale, as a natural or a sharp or a flat. It must, therefore, be called F sharp.

10 If we want to play the scale of G, we must always have F sharps instead of Fs.

scales and keys

Music written using the notes of the scale of G is in the **key** of G major Music is in the key of G if it uses notes taken *in any order* from the scale of G. It will have F sharps in it instead of Fs.

In the same way, music is in the key of C if it takes its notes, in any order, from the scale of C. Music in C major will contain no notes with sharps or flats.

In what keys are the following?:

(a) _____ (b) _____ (c) _____

(d) Write in the sharps needed to make these bars in the key of G

Margin answers:

5 Tone

6 between 3 and 4 and between 7 and top note

7(a) a semitone;
(b) a tone

Answer to Page 24 Questions 14(e)

key signatures

11 It would be inconvenient if a sharp sign had to be entered separately in front of every F in a piece in G major. Instead, we may write an F sharp at the beginning of every stave, immediately after the clef and before the time signature. This is called the **key signature.** Once this is done, all notes written as Fs must be played as F sharps, unless altered by accidentals.

F sharp to G
C sharp to D'

G major key signature

12 Here is the key signature of G major. Notice that though there are two F sharps available in the treble clef, we use the upper one in the key signature.

C major key signature

13 C major has no sharps or flats, so its key signature will be a blank - This is the key signature of C major:

scale of D major

14 Look at the white notes from D to the D' an octave above.

16(a) a semitone
(b) B flat
(c) a semitone

Between D (1) and E (2) there is a tone;
(a) What is the interval between E (2) and F? _____
(b) What should the interval be between the second and third degrees of a major scale? (Remember the TTS T TTS order) _____
(c) What black note must be chosen instead of F? _____

The first three notes of D major are therefore

F sharp (3) to G (4) is a semitone; G (4) to A (5) is a tone; A (5) to B (6) is a tone. All of these intervals are correct.

(d) What is the interval between B (6) and C? _____

We need a tone between 6 and 7 to keep the TTS T TTS pattern
We will have to use C sharp as 7 and not C.
C sharp (7) to top D is a semitone, which is correct.

TEST 9

The notes of D major scale are:

(e) Between which notes are there semitones? _____

Mark them with brackets

D major key signature

15 The key signature of D major is F sharp and C sharp.

F major

16 Look at the white notes from F to the F' an octave above.

There is a tone between the keynote F and G (2).
There is a tone beween G (2) and A (3). Both of these are correct.
(a) What interval is needed between 3 and 4 of a major scale?
(b) What black note must therefore be chosen as 4 in F major?

B flat to C (5) is a tone; C (5) to D (6) is a tone; D (6) to E (7) is a tone.
(c) What interval is E (7) to top F?
The only black note needed in F major is B flat.

The scale of F major is

14
(a) a semitone
(b) a tone
(c) F sharp

F major key signature

17 The key signature of F major is B flat

(d) a semitone

TEST 9

Add accidentals to make these the scales named. Bracket semitones.

(1) D major   (2) F major

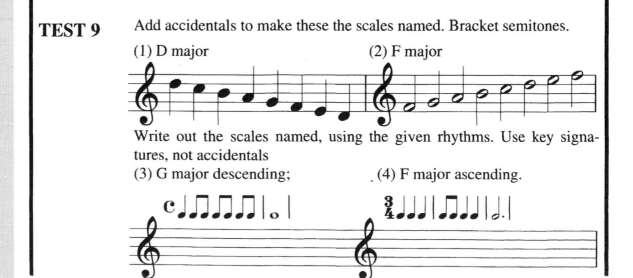

Write out the scales named, using the given rhythms. Use key signatures, not accidentals
(3) G major descending;   (4) F major ascending.

TEST 9
(continued)

Write underneath these key signatures the names of their keys:

(5)   (6)   (7)   (8)

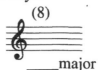

key: _____major   _____major   _____major   _____major

In which major keys are the following phrases?

(9)   Key _____

(10)   Key _____

(11)   Key _____

(12) Put in accidentals to make this in the key of D major:

Give yourself one mark for every correct answer. Write in your score here _____ If it was less than 10, read 12-17 again, and do the test once more.

---

intervals

18   The distance between two notes is called the interval between them.

If the notes of the interval are written one above the other so that they sound at the same time, the interval is called a **harmonic interval**,

If the second note is sounded immediately after the first, the interval is called a **melodic interval.**

Which types of interval, harmonic or melodic, are the following?

(a)   (b)   (c)   (d)

type _____

Answer to Page 26 questions

19 5

TEST 10
1(a) 6th; (b) 3rd;
(c) 4th; (d) 5th;
(e) 7th
2(a) 7th; (b) 2nd
(c) 3rd; (d) 4th; (e) 3rd

3(a)   (b)   (c)

(d)   (e)

TEST 9 (*continued*)
5 G major; **6** D major
7 F major; **8** C major
9 C major; **10** F major

11 Fmajor

12

**measure-
ment of
intervals**

19 The interval is measured by counting the number of degrees between the bottom note and the top note. Include in the counting the bottom and top notes.

Pencil in the degrees of the scale between the outside notes.

How many degrees of the scale are included in the example? _____

There are five degrees of the scale included in the interval, so it is called a fifth.

The intervals you need to know for Grade 1 are a second, a third, a fourth, a fifth, a sixth, a seventh and an octave.

Here are the intervals in C major, with C as the bottom note:

TEST 10 **1** Name these harmonic intervals:

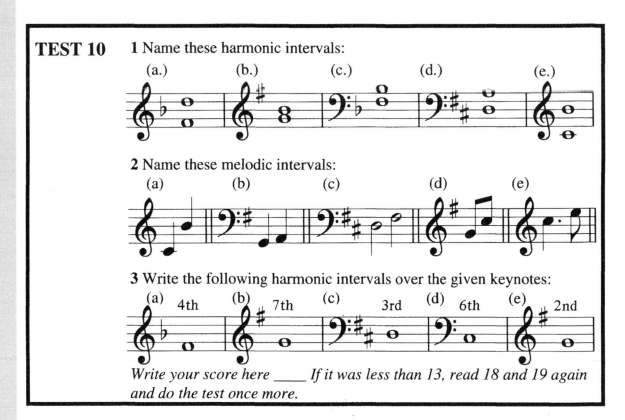

2 Name these melodic intervals:

3 Write the following harmonic intervals over the given keynotes:

Write your score here _____ If it was less than 13, read 18 and 19 again and do the test once more.

tonic triads

20 The keynote of a scale is also called the **tonic** of the scale. This note can be used as the bottom note of a chord of three notes. The other notes used are the third and the fifth of the scale. In C major, therefore, the chord will be made up of the notes C, E and G. The chord is called a **tonic triad.**

All the examples below are tonic triads of C major.

18(a) harmonic;
(b) melodic;
(c) melodic;
(d) harmonic

Answers to questions on this page are in the margin of Page 28

21 What are the notes of the tonic triads of (a.) G major; _____
(b.) D major; _____ (c.) F major? _____

TEST 11

1 Of what major keys are these the tonic triads?

tonic triad of-

(a) _____ (b) _____ (c) _____ (d) _____ (e) _____

2 Write above these tonics the other notes of the tonic triads:

    (a)   (b)   (c)   (d)   (e)

Write your score here _____ If you got less than 8, read 20 and 21 again and do the test once more.

Section 4 - Terms and Signs

A list of the musical terms and signs you need to know for Grade 1 is printed on Page 29. Many terms are sufficiently explained by their English translations.

tempo

1 The speed of a piece is indicated by the tempo instruction, placed at the start of the piece, for example *allegro* for fairly fast.

Look at the tempo markings on Page 29. Write your own list of them arranged in order of speed, starting with the fastest.

_____

changing tempo

2 The Italian term for gradually getting faster is *accelerando*. What word would you use for getting slower gradually? _____

If, after slowing down or getting faster, the music has to return to its original tempo, the instruction *a tempo* is written.

Answers to Page 28 questions

Section 4
4B *fortissimo; forte; mezzoforte; mezzo-piano; piano; pianissimo*

5
(a) ⎯⎯⎯

(b) *decrescendo* or *diminuendo*
(c) ⎯⎯⎯

Answers to Page 28 questions (continued)

6 *staccato*

8(a)

(b)

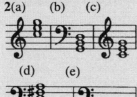
metronome mark

3 Composers often use a type of musical clock called a **metronome** to indicate the exact tempo of beats in a piece. The metronome is set to tick a chosen number of beats per minute. For example, **MM** ♩ **=120** means that the metronome must be set to tick 120 crotchet beats in each minute.

dynamics

4 The word **dynamics** is used to describe the loudness and softness in a piece. Look at the printed list of dynamics on Page 29. Write your own list, putting the loudest on the left and the quietest on the right.

_____

changing dynamics

5 *Crescendo* means gradually getting louder.
(a) Draw the sign for it;
(b) What word which means getting softer? _____
(c) Draw the sign for the word you have chosen in (b)

manner of performance

6 Notes may be played smoothly and joined together - this way of playing is called *legato*. Slurs are placed over or under notes which are to be played in this way.

The last two notes are to be short and detached. which is why there are dots under or over the noteheads. What is this type of playing called?

_____

repeat signs

7 Repeat signs are placed at the beginning and end of the line of music in 6. The line has to be played twice, making a total of 8 bars.

Other signs which make a performer go back and play music again are:

da capo

(a) *da capo* or *(D.C.)* when the performer must go back to the beginning and play until the *fine* mark;

dal segno

(b) *dal segno* or *(D.S.)* when the performer must go back to the sign, written 𝄋 and then play from it just as far as the *fine* mark.

**8va--------
ottava**

8 Notes which come under this sign must be played an octave higher than written. If the sign is written under notes, the notes which are over the bracket must be played an octave lower.

Write out these notes at the pitch they should sound:

Musical Terms & Signs

Tempo:

a tempo	in time (*tempo* means time)
adagio	slow; leisurely
allegro	fairly fast
allegretto	fairly fast, but less fast than *allegro*
andante	at moderate walking pace
lento	slow
moderato	at a moderate speed

Dynamics

forte (f)	loud
fortissimo (ff)	very loud
mezzoforte (mf)	moderately loud
piano (p)	quiet
pianissimo (pp)	very quiet
mezzopiano (mp)	moderately quiet

Changes to Tempo

accelerando	getting faster gradually
rallentando (rall.)	getting slower gradually
ritardando (ritard.) (rit.)	getting slower gradually
ritenuto (rit.)	holding back

Changes to Dynamics

crescendo (cresc.)	gradually getting louder
decrescendo (decresc.)	gradually getting quieter
diminuendo (dim.)	gradually getting quieter

Manner of Performance

cantabile	in a singing style
legato	smoothly
staccato	sharp; detached

Other

da capo (D.C.)	(repeat) from the beginning
dal segno (D.S.)	(repeat) from the sign, 𝄋
fine	end

Qualifying words

molto in front of a word means very, or much. For example, *molto piano* means very quiet.
poco in front of a word means little, or slightly. For example, *poco crescendo* means getting slightly louder.

Signs

            is often used for *crescendo*, (gradually getting louder).

            is often used for *diminuendo*, (gradually getting quieter).

A dot over a note, or under a note, means that the note is to be played staccato.

A > sign over or under a note means that the note must be accented.

The sign ⌢ over or under a note means that the performer should pause on the note.

M.M. is short for Maelzel's Metronome. The performer is to set the metronome to the number which follows. If the direction is, for example MM ♩= 60, it means that there should be sixty crotchet beats to the minute.

8va⸺ over a group of notes means that you must play the marked notes an octave higher . The sign *8va⸺* written under notes means that the notes must be played an octave lower.

A slur over a group of notes means that the notes should be played *legato* - in other words, joined together. Don't confuse this sign with the tie, which links together two notes of the same pitch.

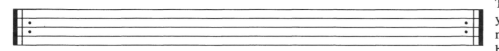

The marks at the end mean that you must go back to the first marks, and repeat the music between the marks..

Answers to questions on Page 30. (a) **3/4** (b) D major; (c) G; (d) *staccato* - play sharply; (e) *legato* - play smoothly; (f) a natural; (g) a crotchet rest, 𝄽 ; (h) fast; (i) get slower; (j) 6 and 7; (k) the notes are the same; (l) *piano* = quiet

Coda – fitting your knowledge together

(*Coda* is the Italian word for a tailpiece – something played at the end of a piece of music.)

Now that you have come to the end of this book, you will be able to understand more about of the pieces of music you play, sing, or compose yourself. .

See if you can answer the questions about this piece. *(Correct answers are on the bottom of Page 29.)*

1. **Allegro**

Le Petit Rien (Couperin)

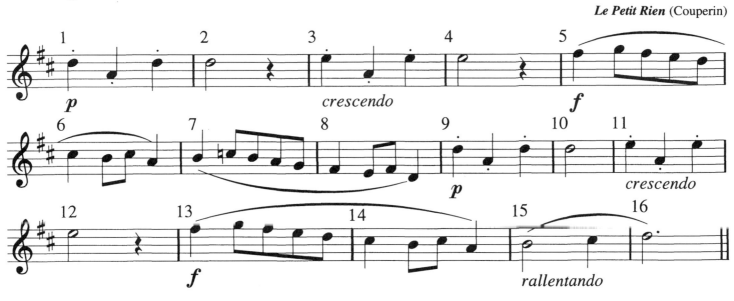

(a) Write in a suitable time signature in bar 1.

(b) In what key does the piece start? _____

(c) What is the letter name of the highest note of the piece? _____

(d) What do the dots mean over the notes in bar 1? _____

(e) What does the slur mean under the notes in bars 7 and 8? _____

(f) What is the name of the type of accidental which is written in bar 7?_____

(g) What is the missing rest in bar 10? Write it in on the music._____

(h) What does the word 'Allegro' mean at the beginning? _____

(i) What does the word *rallentando* mean in bar 15 _____

(j) What degrees of the scale of D major are the notes of bar 15? _____

(k) What do you notice about bars 1 to 4, and bars 9 to 12? _____

(l) What word is *p* short for in bar 1, and what does the word mean in English? _____

Made in the EU